Written on Petals

Elle Amora Dawson

BookLeaf
Publishing

India | USA | UK

Presentation by *BookLeaf Publishing*

Web: www.bookleafpub.com

E-mail: info@bookleafpub.com

ISBN: 9789358318029

First edition 2024

DEDICATION

To all who have ever faded

May you heal and find yourself again

Empty Pages

An empty notebook
Dust settled on the pages
What could it apprise

Elle Amora Dawson

Sorrowful Ashes

Ashes everywhere
Her sorrowful pages burned
She lived beyond them

Elle Amora Dawson

Distorted Beauty

A shattered mirror
Tiny fragments of her heart
Her beauty faded
She sees herself distorted
The key is forever lost

Elle Amora Dawson

His Queen

A crown for his Queen
Embraced with adoration
He yearns in her heart

Elle Amora Dawson

Boldly She Stands

5

Her lipstick is bold
She stands against violence
Her voice captivates

Elle Amora Dawson

Sentiments

She wrote her heartfelt sentiments
In the moments of her distress
To always reflect
To never lose herself
In the midst of her despair

Elle Amora Dawson

Beautiful Matriarch

As a newborn held in her arms
I imprinted on her heart
Holding my hand as a little girl
I always hear her saying
Be a lady
Be eloquent in your words
Be witty if you must
The things she taught me
The passions we shared
Her writing always inspired me
The years had caught up to her
At her bedside
Holding her hand
She too had imprinted on my heart
I looked at her one last time
As she drifted to sleep
She would never truly leave me
The world knew her as Carol Ann Curry

I knew her as my loving Grandmother

She was a beautiful Matriarch

Elle Amora Dawson

Crimson Rose

I buried my name
Reformed in all its beauty
The darkness has left
The skeletons rest in peace

A new crimson rose has bloomed

Elle Amora Dawson

Victoria

In a quaint little village
Close to Roselawn
A beautiful Victorian estate
Called us home
The magnolia trees are in full bloom
In our ambrosial garden
Our love is deeply rooted here
We call our home Victoria

Forever our love lives in the burg

Elle Amora Dawson

Veiled Garden

Her lips stay soundless
Pain disguised in her garden
Her face is still veiled
She'll never bare her true soul
The beast still lives among her

Elle Amora Dawson

Songbird

Beautiful in her own light
Her words are written on petals
Her voice awakens my soul
She is my songbird

Forever the sonnet of my heart

Elle Amora Dawson

Phantom

The night sky falls
Her dreams are haunted
By the phantom of her past
She waits for a ray of light
To release her
A new day dawns

Elle Amora Dawson

You

You will never
Consume any space in my heart
You will never
Be a thought in my mind
You will never
Define any part of me
You are erased
Banished from my being

I am gone

Forever free from you

Elle Amora Dawson

Ink

Dearest of them all
She wrote her whole life in ink
Because it mattered
Sincerely in black

Elle Amora Dawson

Timeless

A timeless suitcase for her vintage soul
Tattered and torn
Much like her heart
She carries her history
She searches to mend it all
Embellished pens for her postcards
Pretty paper for her junk journals
All tucked away

She's going places

Her journey begins

Elle Amora Dawson

Boudoir

So lavish and lush
The entire room smells of
peony flowers and soft perfume
Silk in every corner
A beautiful makeup vanity
Where she brushes colors to her face
Like painting a canvas
Fancy fashion magazines
Circles and stars around her dreams
Records scattered
Of her favorite music
She lets down her hair
Her emotions flow out

She writes in her most private room

Invitation only

Elle Amora Dawson

Typewriter

There on the writing desk
So much character
A beautiful seductive black
Scarlet ribbon
Her typewriter
Waiting for her fingertips

Elle Amora Dawson

Love Warrior

All the sudden
Her happiness
Made the sadness dissipate
Her love conquered every battle
A true warrior
Who survived it all

Elle Amora Dawson

Keeper

I don't want to leave
Keep me here in this feeling
Pull me in closer

Elle Amora Dawson

Sophisticated

All to herself
She is interesting
The kindness in her eyes
Her defined cheekbones
Dressed in black and white
Her gray suede heels
She is sexy and chic
Soft around all her edges
She is completely sophisticated
Everything gravitates to her
She has no clue of her beauty
She is bona fide

Elle Amora Dawson

Delicately Flawed

Delicate and flawed
It was never easy for her
She changed everything
She was worth every moment

She is a statement of strength

Elle Amora Dawson